For Clare Farrow

THE DOUBLE-ENDED KEY

with many thanks

?!/—/⊥℃4

All best wishes

Roy Davids

GW00368188

Roy

Acumen Publications
2011

ACKNOWLEDGEMENTS are due to the following publications in which some of these poems have appeared: *Acumen, The Epic Poise,* 1999, *East of Auden,* 2003, *Oxford Magazine, White Noise,* 2006, *Poems for Children,* 2009, *Earth Moon (website dedicated to Ted Hughes),* 2010, *Initiate: New Oxford Writing,* 2010, *First Sixty: The Acumen Anthology,* 2010.

Copyright © Roy Davids 2011
Cover illustration © Amand Brookes and Ken Adlard 2011.

British Library C-i-P data:
A catalogue record for this book is
available from the British Library.

ISBN: 978 - 1 - 873161 - 27 - 2

Published by
ACUMEN PUBLICATIONS
6 The Mount
Higher Furzeham
Brixham
South Devon
TQ5 8QY
UK

CONTENTS

White Noise   7

Fish / Fishing   8

The Music   9

Red Kite / Silent Movie   10

A Time for All Seasons   11

Memories, Reflections, Gratitudes   12

Sixteen Telegrams to Ted   17

On Being Told a Crow Knocked   20

Her Voice Is / Invitation   21

The Scent of a Woman / Hearing her Smile   22

Modest Proposal   23

Humble Advice from a Picture   24

Redacted Poem   25

On my Portrait of T.S. Eliot   26

The Double-Ended Key   27

Scansion   28

View over the village churchyard   29

Bed-Fellow   30

Being / Indecision   32

The Parachute of the Soul   33

Analysand   34

Inflation   37

The Auctioneer   38

Manuscript Poem   40

Southern Spain   41

San Expedito   42

Wilder Thame   44

Keeper's Cottage, Great Haseley   45

The Power of Poetry   46

40   47

Wild Goose   48

Bee   49

Tulips   50
Autumn Coming / Killing Field   51
Nature Notes   52
Winter Trees   53
Moment   54
The Sacred Peepal Tree / Peace   55
Sagacities   56
Night-time / Peacock at Newnham Courtenay Arboretum   57
At the Dentist   58
Advert   59
Anasyrma   60
Undressing Fruit   61
Getting to Know you   62
Father   65
Mother   69
Note to Father and Mother   81
In Memoriam Bettina Bachmann   83
RIP R.A.   84
The Day of Ted's Funeral   85
Doubting Thomases   86

ROY DAVIDS was formerly Head of the Department of Printed Books and Manuscripts at Sotheby's and also Marketing Director, Head of Communications and Company Strategist there. Before then he was a teacher, historian, and cataloguer for an antiquarian bookseller. Since leaving Sotheby's he was a dealer in manuscripts and portraits of artistic people on his own account until 2006. He is author of *Provenance: Collectors, Dealers and Scholars in the Field of Chinese Ceramics in Britain and America*, 2011, a pamphet of poems, *White Noise*, Acumen 2006, and articles on manuscripts and related subjects, portraits and Ted Hughes. He is a collector of prose and poetical manuscripts, portraits and porcelain.

For Miss P., RIP

White noise

Shostakovitch had a special friend
whom he could telephone to come
and spend some time with him.
No words would pass between them;
they'd just sit silently across the room:
Shostakovitch solid as in his photograph.
After half an hour, he would thank
the friend, who'd then get up and leave.
What he needed was the company,
not conversation; just not to be alone;
to have the sense of someone being there.
Perhaps it was telepathy? A transference
back and forth? A therapy? Sounds
outside our human reach and range?

Most of what elephants communicate
we feel but cannot hear; it is too deep
for us, though they can pick it up ten miles away.
We do not hear white noise, but know it's there,
covering over silence – like dust in air,
only seen in sunlight. It protects us,
and our inner lives;
in part allows our sense of self.

Often less than music half unheard,
because not really listened to;
lighter than laughter through a wall
or children in the gardens down the hill;
it's like a picture not noticed till removed;
can be as slight as half the senses; a feeling –
almost beyond the rim of consciousness.

We seek out that comfort as our norm –
need a pulse of sympathy out there.
Silence can leave us anxious

empty
too aware.

Might much of what is meant by love
be best described as noise that's white?

Fish

They are the jewels
of the necklace of water.

They are the pearls
of the deeper pools.

They are the diamonds
in the waterfall's hair.

Fishing

They lay like a broken mirror
in the bottom of the boat
as if the surface of the lake
had fallen from its frame
and we had gathered splinters
of the silvered glass.

The Music

slowly lifts its head
from the middle of the orchestra;
silently commanding, eyes half closed.
Temples tighten. Mouths go dry.
The air focuses like a buddha,
ready to receive its votaries.

The orchestra sways to its partner's
lead and together they enter the dance.
Music can lift and fall like wind,
sweep across landscapes, fondle
fields, lick along the lines of bays,
filter the sea through its fingertips.

Or sit gossiping on a wall.
Wise, it will philosophise,
nag at a single tone or theme.
Brash, it is a hurdy gurdy band.
Gentle, it can slip into a waltz.
Sad, it turns away, and weeps.

I like music that wants to press
my cheek against its shoulder,
music so affectively refined,
it seems like water falling.
High on this side of silence,
made from a skein of sighs.

Red Kite

over the Haseleys

Describe your circles in the sky,
Oxfordshire eagle. Sail the thermal
tides. Soar; bank; hover; wheel;
show your rudder's skill. Flex your
finger-feathers; stretch out full span –
put back an edge on nature,
too ironed and trimmed by Man.

So gentle bird, weak of talon,
swooping down for carrion,
mobbed by your little cousins.
Yet, it is hard to sing like Shelley now,
the days of Angels seem quite dead,
but my spirits rise religious when I see
the flash of your rusty undersides,
and you glide, and float, and whistle.

Silent Movie

for L.O.

The sky is flawless cobalt,
though leaves, burnt orange,
shake wildly in the bitter wind.
Everything is crisp –
new snow, twigs underfoot,
all conversation.
The day insists on itself
and those who venture out
melt into something marvellous
like birds' silhouettes
dipping silently in the lake.

A Time for All Seasons

back from Peggs Farm, along Latchford Lane, Great Haseley

October early evening sun,
low in a cradle of crimson cloud,
illuminates the yellow
in those greens that slowly fade
and enamels savoury
all the russets and browns.
Earth, freshly turned,
smacks delicious with its tang
of Aga bread and cats' paws.
Fields are rastafarian
corduroy, or lightly blushing green
in the anti-cycle Spring
of the second annual crop.

Birds overhead rehearse formations,
check their ancient charts,
retell exotic travelling tales.
Some waddle, out of depth on land,
or take off like propeller planes –
old crows' engines falter on approach
and ducks come down on their petrol tanks.

As the Earth turns,
Autumn reaches for a coat,
and Summer, out late,
hurries home to hibernate.
Rain forecasts itself
in peninsulas of cloud.
The air practices its bite.
Candles are lit
in the great cathedral
– angels tune their instruments
– the west doors close.
The world slips back
before words and language.
The service of remembrance begins.

Memories, Reflections, Gratitudes, 1998 and later:

A celebration of Ted Hughes

Levelling the air out with his hand,
his huge handsome head held low,
watching me caught in the spiral of words,
living again his own first thrill,
bringing out the marvel of it all –
it was the way he made things magical.
Partly it was his childlike sense,
his boyish charged excitedness,
as in our two days at the zoo
when, asked to be a wildebeest,
he made a tiger turn and snarl.
He paid court to a cockatoo,
and was a gibbon gibbon.
That great roar of laughter –
like his cry for Ha and Golding,
rippling round the rafters.
The way he ruminated over food,
as if an antique mystic thought
passed over in some foreign fare.
Or watching, from his own armchair,
him rewriting Ovid on his knee,
the words just running from his pen,
under the half dim table light,
while we buffooned upon the floor.
Or as he simply sat and read,
rubbing his shingled eye.
Later, out on a walk with him,
falling in with his rise and fall;
it was the way he moved the mud
to let trapped water out to play.
Or, set a subject, as we set out,
with what mastery he wrought it,

endlessly engaging and engaged.
Then, those long drifting drives round Devon,
sometimes at a funeral pace,
reading new poems while he drove along,
questioning what this or that one meant.
We sketched out thirty books and schemes,
testing titles, shouting down the wind,
and piled the dirt on poets, politicians, friends.
He showed me all his ancient haunts,
and his folks me, in Devon and in York,
including the great Aunt Hilda,
and, in time, to most of those he knew
promoting me as agent and as friend.
Then, there was his quite distinctive style
of leaning over bridges, his Barbour
hooked on his right-hand index finger,
guaging how high the water was,
half turned, one foot just off the ground,
pointing at fish I could not see.
And that day of mackerel and bream
when the pressure fell below the graph
and, only just, we got inside the bar, then,
back home, babbled like ancient mariners.
Calling, merely for a chat.'What's new?
What's happened? Who's with who?'
or a thin message on the answer phone:
'It's only Ted; how are you?
I'll try the other line'.
Oh, we put the world to rights,
ripped up some reputations,
launched high gossip at the ether.
Unnumbered rides to restaurants;
police-slow drives, to music, home;
the joy of quaffing rich mens' wine,
revelling in the sheer indulgence of it all.
Three muscateers: Carol, Ted, and me,

raising a glass to luck, and love, and us.
Late mornings; he was always late for meals.
Then our plans for merchant ventures –
trousers; shares; antiques; student lets –
him flirting with ideas, new explanations,
History was for living, not to learn,
scholars could keep the record right,
Magic's in a seance, saga, eagles' flight.
And yet how much his history was him.
One secret was the way he'd concentrate,
that word so early – adverbially –
in the famous fox he thought,
searching out the inner spirit,
the *duende*, of each thing.
His will to share his world;
to teach, to open up horizons,
making them what you most desired;
like being converted at your own front door.
He opened up so many things for me,
taught me how to train my mind,
and even how to fall asleep.
How wonderful the memories are
of all the pleasures that we shared:
of the bowl of light we once raised high upon a Devon hill;
or the angel that did truly fly on a wall in Gloucestershire.
The mighty hand that clasped electric when we met or went,
and his big slow bull-like turn back into home,
captured in my mirror as I inched out of the lane.
The seance we attended at his healer's house
with foolish women and two flickering lamps
unsure about the good bits, or the fraud
who conjured up wild voices and events.
The walks down rivers, Nature murmuring,
content; our London lives beneath the radar.
Grateful also for your pheromonal smell;
for wild outbursts (letting off your steam);
for being so entirely free with me.
I loved your love of silence

and of the dusk and dawn;
your bible bond with Nature
and the sacred drama of the earth.
Your lion's eye; the hare bone in your ear,
the crush and crashing of the bear.
Your vast capacious mind,
that temple of your inner life;
as visionary, your cell.
The depth of your response,
your heightened sense,
your tact, your quite especial care.
The momentary jealousies;
the human flare.
And then your deep forgiveness.
For fishing; though I failed.
For having seen you cast
like Merlin laying on a spell.
For your passionate dispassion,
your sympathy; your courage;
your compassion.
For your legendary discretion,
and all the times you let me in.
Thank you for your fears about the world
and your dedication to yourself;
for your balance of perfection,
and powerful pursuit of it. For the thrill
of hearing that I'd done a good thing well.
I learned your sense of right and wrong
and felt you wait for me to grow aware.
I am in awe of your Shakespearean mind,
the great arc of your intellect,
your sacred talent and your skill,
the mingled music of your voice –
like God auditioning for Man.
Your wisdom and your love of life,
your way with words and metaphor,
your subtle insights and imagining,
your 'gusto', energy, and power.

The letters that lit up my days;
poems that made my mind fly free;
prose that forced the bended knee.
Your writing, an uncoiling spring,
only matched in manuscripts by Bach.
You were a purpose in my life;
a solid rock of reference;
still yet a presence in your empty chair.
You were loaned out by the gods,
retained their epic poise,
to see the cosmic broadbrush myth
and make mere men rejoice
at the complex complicatedness
of the spirit and the mind.
You were a seer, shaman, friend;
Coleridge-cum-Wordsworth – and Yourself.
A loss to Art, you have diminished life
for those you leave bereft behind.
But it is one function of the great
to force on us the contradiction
of whether more to celebrate the work
or lament the life's extinction.
For now, I'll touch on simple benefactions,
on favours unconditionally done,
on comradeship and love assumed,
on your kindness, and for being shy.
And most perhaps for letting me be there,
and being so uniquely mine,
as in other ways, each quite unique,
you touched the lives of many men,
bringing out the best in them.
Your friendship was a miracle to me.
I really cannot comprehend
all that mighty heart is lying still.

Sixteen Telegrams to Ted

1
A bird was singing:
you studied it –
concentratedly –
going about your business.

2
You and Seamus
sang in the front of the car
on the way to the airport.
Singing heads.

3
New Year's Day
on Hartland Head
we cupped the unseasonable sun
in our hands for a photograph.

4
We lay out on the ground
for our photograph:
sardines in a tin.
When it came out
we were corpses
in a Saxon grave.

5
Lying in the sun
on the riverbank
the cows came to investigate.
A post-Plathian event.

6
My black cat
sat on your mat.
You called her
a hole in the carpet.

7
When I told you that
she'd come in through her flap
looking like a victim of rape
I saw your shutter click twice.

8
You drove 400 miles
to take me home
post-operatively.
It probably cost the world
a poem. I didn't care.

9
Going to Ireland
we met Catherine Ann
and were speaking to Seamus
about Shakespeare.
She asked her father
if she knew him as well
having met quite a lot
who were famous.

10
The stream down the lane
was lit by the moon.
I walked behind
on a stairway to heaven.

11
Your healer
waved his hands
at my gouty finger.
'Do you feel that heat?'
'No, just the wind.'
That cost a fiver.

12
The waitress had stockings
and generous thighs.
She swished quite loudly
each time she walked by.

13
When we both said
we read out words
aloud in our head
we looked at each other
as you might at a brother.

14
When you talked
at table,
you could have made
the table talk.
It preferred to listen.

15
Of course it was partly
your father and mother.
But for you it was also
your sister and brother.

16
You loved to read aloud in Spanish
because it was so beautiful.
She loved to hear you read in Spanish
because it was so beautiful.

On being told that a Crow knocked at Ted Hughes's window early in the morning

Rat tat.
Rat tat.

Sleep no more
for I have murdered sleep
at cock crow.

Rat tat.
Rat tat.

Raven speak no more
I am now in paradise
pranked upon the hewn lyre.

Rat tat.
Rat tat.

You stole my birthright
and have sold my song
for some worldly carry-on.

Rat tat.
Rat tat.

I place my feet about your eyes
and crown you crow bar none.
Come King Crow. Come croaking.

Her voice is

music caught on the breeze
in a sheltered garden,
mid-afternoon lapping warm;
easy sigh of summer scent,
apple, honeysuckle, rose;
eyes dipped against the sun;
a distant clip of horses' hooves
finger-touch word endings;
a silver scarf falling.

Invitation

You do not know how much
the silky wind can calm
when it whispers in the palm trees
or turns the sleeping sea
to glittering diamonds
on a star-clear night
off a Greek island.
Come with me and see.

The Scent of a Woman

for Angela Patti in Sicily

Your message, as from an ocean-island,
or music held suspended on the air,
shimmered from your skin, a jasmine whisper,
the dying fall of a summer evening's sigh.
Mysterious, mellow-velvet, cool,
it spoke in promises and riddles
like women dressing a princess
for an occasion so special
the secret was sealed in a spell.
The dream wrapped itself
in a cloud or mantle,
vanished in a scented mist,
and came back as an Angel.

Hearing her smile

Of course with a woman
who has a scent like yours
you can also hear her smile,
though we say laughter.
What tinkling peals of Sicily's
delight so late at night!
My dreams will be of little bells
to a slow shoe shuffle of the sea.

Modest Proposal

Take the communion of my hand,
the laying on of hands –
my hand in holiness on yours,
– palm measuring palm –
yours shy in the shade of mine.
My hand's healing whisper
sends a tremulous message
along the songlines of your life.
More ancient and ceremonial
than speech, touch is the ritual
in supplication's art.

There is a formal consecration
in the choreography of hands.

Benedicamur.
Benedicamur.

Give me your hand,
so I can ask for it.

Humble Advice
from a Picture

Do not hang me
over heat
or from my feet
I'll go dry and thin
like aging skin

Do not hang me
in the light
or then I might
fade away and die
just like a sigh

Redacted Poem

On my portrait of T.S. Eliot by Gerald Kelly, now sold

I go into your room
now you're no longer there,

presiding like an altar piece,
high on the furthest wall.

For more than thirty years
you'd looked down on me.

One eye had reproval as its mote;
the other had redemption.

Now I have neither magistrate,
nor the needy mendicant.

I ceased to need you –
psychologically.

The Double-Ended Key

Adolphus Frederick,
Duke of Cambridge,
tenth child of George III,
had a double-ended key,
each end like a Chinese seal.
They turned the locks
on the two royal parks
of which he was the Ranger.
Though partly ceremonial,
and his official badge as well,
it meant he only took one key
when he went to do his job.
Crossing the road between the parks,
he merely switched the ends around.
It had a certain elegance.
I now have that double-ended key
though it has no useful purpose
except to carbonize the thought
that the locks we have inside
are better served by two keys
cut on a single shaft.

Scansion

Mining today seemed to be
in a bell pit with a narrow seam.
Slid in on a stretcher, my nose
just inches from the roof.
All around the clank and crash
of industry, like blacksmiths
pounding iron bars and water
thrown on white-hot metal.
Ghostly factories ringing with
remembered agonies and echoes
shuddering the crazed cacophony
of a man-made brutal beast.
Beethoven and Mozart filtered
through my brain with orders
not to move – this one will be
six minutes, you may feel a cold
sensation in your arm. Dazed,
I was drawn out an hour later,
sure I'd been underground,
had relived the sense and sound
of that vast inhuman revolution
whose ends were morals to its means.

View over the village churchyard

Swindon Village, Gloucestershire

She comes each day
to tidy up his room,
make the bed, smooth
it out with loving hands
tracing his presence
as if he's really there.
The mark he left
endures so strong,
it's a scent about the place,
and she can see his laughter
as a halo round his hair.
He is her one and constant joy,
though she can be sorely vexed –
by things that change,
and those that stay the same.

She dusts and polishes and cleans,
freshens up the flowers,
gets everything just right.
Then she sits, abstracted,
near his dormitory bed,
seeming to dream about
the way things were
and what she should
have said. He is the son
she'd waited for, and once
again she waits upon.
But now he also waits
for her. It's time for her to go.
They lock the churchyard up
on the stroke of eight o'clock.

Bed-Fellow

for Pushkin, *who was a dear friend, or had the acquaintance, of T. H. OM, C.O.H, Sir S. S., Leonard B., Basil B., Charles C., Alan S., Ruth F., S. H.NL, Charles and Brenda T, the Morps, T. and G.P., Grey and Neiti, John and Gina Wilson, Amanda, Paul, Tad, and Lydia Brookes-Forty, Michael and Jill Brookes, the Hambidges (Lucy, Roger, Ben, George and Evie), Lisa Cox, Dominic Jellinek, Kathy Leab, Kenneth Rendell, Felix Pryor, Joan Winterkorn, Desmond and Fiona Heyward, Richard Griggs, Samuel and Jennifer Stein, Sophie Dupré, Desmond and Alice Laurence, Michael and Patty Naxton, Alan Rawlings, Paul Reeves, Mike and Maria Spink, Jonathan Langley, Jos Evans, Lucinda Orr, Peter and Mary Isaac, Julie Armstrong-Donaghy (whose lap she loved and who, like her servant/master, she trusted, absolutely), Tessa Milne-Escarzaga-Chesters (whose computer and work she often shared; it is rumoured that there is extant a correspondence between Miss P and Miss T), and many others of the foremost literary, convivial and artistic men and women of the time* — this partly in imitation of a biography of D.G. Rossetti's wombat, named Top, written for the *Dictionary of National Biography* and signed J.S. [? William James Stillman], but not published there, found among the posthumous papers of Sir Leslie Stephen, the editor of the *DNB*. Top, perhaps formerly the companion of Prince Alfred, Duke of Edinburgh, had had the acquaintance of Mr James Whistler, Mr William Rossetti, Miss Christina Rossetti and Sir Edward Burne-Jones and was known 'to sleep on the épergne in the middle of the dinner table'; Puskin, a Devonian by origin (and therefore possibly of Moorish descent), while similarly good-natured, was of a more sophisticated race, and had the most exquisite and courtly manners: see John Simons, *Rossetti's Wombat*, 2008.`

I wake with a purple pressure,
like an ember, in my head. It's
the velvet sort of ache you get
from dozing after dinner, or
when you leave the heating on
and go, forgetful, up to bed.
She slips in like the shadow
of a sigh; switches on the engine
of her smile, a sort of self-hypnosis
that does for counting or the candle's
Chinese eye. Gradually her murmur
melts in a solicitude of silence
that lets our souls confide, metred
only by my breathing, with spaces
twice her size. The pressure lifts,
the ember dies, and she slides us
to that one place in the world, where
the one without becomes the one inside.

Being

I think therefore I am
is good enough for me.
But what is true of you? –
could you be the figment
of a fiction that is me?
Because you think, you are,
but then, therefore, am I?
By thinking all I can
about a thing, and finding
that we don't agree, I sense
the difference that is us,
the difference of identity,
which makes you, therefore, you,
and therefore let's me be.

Indecision

It's rarely the generalities of life
that stand out or mean
anything real or particular.
It's the details –
the corner of a smile,
a half movement, a sense
of something, rather than itself,
that can be thrilling, though
not always willing an action.
And in its nervous indecision,
whole worlds, entire realities,
do not occur, or experiences happen –
but thoughts and dreams can hint at them.
Life is half-lit, and potentialities
remain transfixed between
a division of indifferent blues.

The parachute of the soul

for Julia Rendell

To forgive we must forget
To forget we must recall
To remember we select
In selecting we sense all
By sense we understand
The reason we explain
By explaining we revive
And make experience live
So as we close we open
And when we open close
Out of pain we thrive
Fragmented we are whole

Analysand

For J.S.

Without a doubt the world is brighter –
meaning it is less dim as well
as being whiter. The mixture of mist
and patchy fog that is depression
comes and goes, but in a way
less dense and overwhelming.
That I should find myself 'of interest'
could be concerning if it wasn't such
a gain. Before, I didn't care if I
survived, though suicide itself,
if entertained, was really not an option;
it was flirted with, somewhat indulged,
– it is an answer that ignores the question,
damaging most those left behind.
To say I am of interest to myself
involves a sense that the complexity
of man is greater than my mood allowed
before, but also that I have the will
to find in it a stimulus. I saw myself
as fairly one-dimensional, unifaced;
even, to be frank, a fraud and boring;
operating on the margins of my life,
running my finger round its rim.
Now an inner dialogue is going on
nearly all the time. Those questions, which
in the past, would certainly have terrified,
now have a currency, and there is
an urgent need to have them satisfied;
to spend, not save, to waste some time.
It is as if my appetite had vanished
and come back. A parallel is when
I first wore glasses and the world
attained real depth, began to shine.

Other people are starting to exist
outside of me, to be exciting
for themselves, not exclusively a threat,
things from which I feel an urge to hide.
Instead they have become significant
because they *are* so different, no longer
merely objects to have in my control.
They still speak a language that is strange,
but with a music that is easy on the ear.
Could I kiss joy as it swings on by?
– a thought unthinkable a year or so ago.
Let's hope it lasts. Even the odd day
down doesn't get so out of hand; I think
I can see it now as being just a patch –
one day when the defences build on back
or a time when some weird experiment
takes place inside my body or my brain.
It's less of a catastrophe, less total, blind.
It's just a setback. Life and the journey
don't always travel in the straightest lines.
So there are days when the system goes
on down; the power fails; the hard drive
clears. But I know the supervisor's
number now. The future has regained
a sense of promise, the unknown is no
longer a decline. To find I have some inner
life, not strife, is a tremendous gain.
Before, I was driven, self-accused,
seriously despised; now I have a real desire
to know myself, to clear away the falsity,
be honest, straight, sometimes perhaps
a little wiser to myself. I want to live,
not just exist because I have to. The threat
of not managing evaporates; pleasure,
enjoyment, even happiness, feel as
if they could be mine. I have not made

the journey yet, but I want it to begin,
find a place not just behind my eyes.
I have some hope I could be whole,
maybe even grow. I used to only show,
not share; scored off others,
though to win against myself –
that has not changed, but there's a will
to mend that break inside. I have lived
too much of life in mourning, things
have been black-edged, and I had to filter
all experience, ensure that content
lacked emotion, was kept out of the core.
One way some things have changed
is that they're more direct, my access
to them seems to be less sieved by me.
Music can enter in without a pass,
words may have lost their need to please
in the sense of to impress. To turn again
at the corner of the stair, to turn again,
to share things with myself, reflect,
not add, account, not need to hurry past.
There is some sense of subtle change
of medium, from film to live theatre,
meaning it is more real, maybe even better.
I am less self-prescriptive, have found
in me a person with whom I can converse.

Inflation

Time hath my wallet in his hand
and spends too freely from my store.
Each pound is for his pleasure,
and fifty is for more.

My stash expands its rubber band,
but cash you can't insure.
Each pound that leaves my treasure,
feels lighter than before.

Years and days are grains of sand,
so Futures won't mature,
now Time's no more a measure,
and more is only more.

The auctioneer

steps up to the rostrum
like the priest into his pulpit,
the holy book of bids
open on the lectern.

He looks down upon his flock
with their faith in what he sells,
seeking silence and awed faces
before he will begin.

Intoning legal phrases,
he locks the room in stillness
as though his congregation.
'The first is number 1' - - -

It could have been a hymn
had he gone in for the calling
imagined by his mother
when he took the bingo as a boy.

But now he climbs a stairway
of figures not of souls,
renting out his avocation
instead of rendering to God.

He made his lifetime choice
because he always thought
the power of the auction house
was greater than the Lord's.

And so it is (according to conditions
their lawyers have laid down).
Priests and gods are limited
to old indulgences and prayers,

but he can take and cancel bids;
make demands, entice, cajole,

or even look away (should a debtor
dare to raise an eyebrow – or a hair).

He can animate the chandelier
or find new bidders on the walls.
He charges twice for what he does
though buyers have no rights at all.

He can remove the person
who shouts or flouts the law,
and castigate in tones
that once had parishes in thrall

when priests were placed
above the salt, and businessmen
were fed in kitchens at the back,
not welcomed in the Hall.

Better than God or priest
our auctioneer may be,
tho' he *cannot* value what he sells
or he'd purchase it himself.

And he shows he doesn't know
the price of any thing
by consigning others' goods
to the laps[es] of the gods.

Manuscript Poem

I did not meet you at a party,
exchanging niceties across
the hubbub of a room

or at a dinner, craning out
across the table as you turned
between those seated either side.

Instead, I am the witness, unobserved,
as you reveal your inner self
to friends; the one who sees you

grapple with an archetype
or half-refined idea;
in conflict for control

of notions running live
like electric current down your arm,
the pen in automatic gear.

Or I see you deep in thought,
as you craft the perfect line,
shifting to resolve a crux.

I sit with my best friends –
like you, they mostly are long dead –
their practices and papers open.

Southern Spain

for Ruth

Noon sun burns high, retracting
shadows; colours are bled,
and the landscape becalmed.
Later, the slant discriminates,
perspective filters, and green
rebalances the sea.

Threadbare and curly, hillsides
are bulls' hides. Mountains
conspire under camouflage.
Terraces are neatly knitted.
Bushes stand in ermine rows
like nipples on a prunt cup.

Man plants his own stars –
crooked cruciforms, clumsy
on tiptoe, that seem to semaphore
against the clock and agitate the air
like beating wings, throbbing
the land with urban discontent.

San Expedito, Menorca,

the home of Andrew and Hannah Hankey

dated O three O two O one.

The tiny fields, swept back
to their own margins, are
furnished with carpets
of winter feed, fringed
about by buttercups that
also lap along the lane –
like confetti brushed aside.
A fig tree has fossilised
an octopus; an olive tree
is naked but is still alive.
A horse laughs, a dog
nags at its chain. The sun
which has dispensed
its medicine all day
closes its door behind the hill
and the valley seems to sigh.
The fire and the furnace
fixed, evening descends
like a mist of quietness,
and the terrace starts
to yawn. Menorca slips
into memory and sleep,
life is domestic, small
and self-contained. The valley
seems filled with holy water
for the sanction of the night.
The tide turns between opposites
and sinks down to be the same.
Freed from all its urgent
causes, San Expedito
mutes its bell, and
floats away on dreams.

When God was playing
with his toys, before Time
was even Ancient, he copied
Botticelli's Tuscan hills,
painted in broad swathes
the darker greens of trees,
stacked and scattered stones,
and, wiping out his brush,
he formed the bays. Then,
just about to turn away,
with one deft touch, he
finished off his play, adding
your valley like a signature.
But, more perhaps a matrix
than a word – an authentic
thumbprint of the Lord.

Wilder Thame

Saturday, 30 September

Thame in Oxfordshire, today,
was off at the seaside –
had a hurdy gurdy air.
Not that there was any bunting,
music, circus rides, or fair.
It was as if a pretty girl
was floating through the town
with ribbons in her hair.
A weaving texture
in the light, like dimpled water,
was refracting something,
though nothing was aware.
A late summer sun,
began to glare, exhausted –
with a brighter, whiter light –
straining its resources.
Something salty got
into the quality of air.
A single skein of coolness:
Autumn was running
its fingers through my hair.

Keeper's Cottage, Great Haseley, Spring 2010

down past the War Memorial

'The road to Little Haseley's closed.
We've got a thatch on fire,'
the fireman manning the barricade
across the road, explained.
For three days and two nights
they fought it and stood guard
over the smouldering wreck
in case it was playing possum.
It took ten fire crews and engines
with water tanked from Aylesbury
and the contents of the post-modern
pool of the local Manor House
to finally extinguish it.

The fenced-off carcase
stands as its own memorial,
fixed in a rictus grin.

Now, it's summer: the garden
sports a stand of ruby roses,
and a harlequin balloon,
a big fig, floats by,
belching flames, and roaring.

The Power of Poetry

My builder's
got a silent daughter.
Give her a Coca Cola
and she drinks it.
Give her an apple
and she eats it.
Give her a pound,
and she palms it.
All without
a word or sound.
Then I read her
a poem by Edward Lear,
and, she laughs –
upjamboriously.

40

More perhaps it is at 40
that you wish you'd been more naughty
when naughtiness was just pure daring
and came before the time of caring
who and why and what you were.
It's both a time to stand, and stir.
Really it's such a funny age –
the fire's still in but doesn't rage
so much with vigour – that's a bother.
It's neither one thing nor another:
no longer young; but not yet old,
no wisdom yet; but much less bold.
You think you're still a rated blade
yet certainty begins to fade
as aches and pains deny a passion
and you condemn the latest fashion.
So now that I am nearly 40
perhaps I should be much more naughty
and catch up on all the things I've missed
and kiss all those I haven't kissed.
Or should I be much more mature,
pretend I'm confident and sure,
emulate the wise and slow,
and watch the world just come and go?
Or can I be myself at last
and cull some comfort from the past –
both sinned against as well as sinning –
as lines hatch in and hair is thinning,
and know the good, the wise and naughty
all feel the same about reaching 40?

Wild goose

the lesser concorde,
swoops above the house
yelping and barking,
his neck outstretched,
aimed in concentration
like a dam-buster pilot
at the pond a mile away.

The farmer finishes the poem
with a bang and a whimper
some yelping and barking
and a cutlery clatter.

Bee

Denning Road, Hampstead,
for Professor Desmond and Mrs Alice Laurence

The lilies in the hall
trumpeted their presence,
exuding procreation
with a scent as heady as
a pheromone. Gaudy in
their summer things, they
remind me of a woman
carefree and dangerous.

A bee was found in the
keyhole, in a passion of
desperation and despair.
From the huge world
out there, it had found
that tiny target, enflamed by
the female in the flower.
Let go, it flew away, but

back it came, and was
there again, on your return
later in the day. Wiser now,
it scuttled away, seething,
while I struggle for words
to preserve it forever:
embalmed and bejewelled
deep in an amber forest.

Tulips

How you stare,
eyeing me from
your corner
– so flirtatiously.

Brash little tarts,
clamouring
and calling,
– so outrageously.

Ruby-eyed hussies,
baring your bosoms;
flapping your skirts
– so vampishly.

Blousy old girls
you wake up
in the morning,
– so drowsily.

You're the mermaids
of my garden.

Autumn coming

along the road to Thame

This morning is mediaeval,
mist lies out on the fields
like a blanket of smoking cloud
wrinkling in the tucks and dips,
folding round cattle half asleep
under a sheet of glistenimg dew.
Traffic streams by –
but some, like you,
as from the corner of your eye,
shudder an ancient *dejà vu.*

Killing Field

down Latchford Lane and beyond, Great Haseley

The field left fallow
has been sprayed with death
– pink breath on moleskin
touched with golden sprays.

Nature Notes

looking towards Malvern

A lazy sun gently poaches
against an onyx sky –
silky pink, duck-egg blue,
faded Art-Deco green.
Long lines of exhausted cloud,
patchy white and grey,
trail wistful country tunes
through the upheld hands
of winter trees. The organist
slides in along his settle;
the cellos swell and violins
pizzicato peck like birds
each separate speck of rain.
Piccolos pause to look around
with big cat caution. I walk on
mesmerized by the pageant
that shows as a rolling advert
on the wide-screen western sky.
And marvel at the ingenuity
and skill of the lighting engineer.

Winter Trees

thinned out like fennel hair,
filigree, frail and trembling,
trees by the roadside –
trimmed on the overhang
some way off symmetry –
rest back on shooting sticks.
Those right on the road,
shell-shocked by the noise,
struggle with their hair nets
or hold up hands to ears
against the crumpling blast.
Trees on the inner edge
of fields, exercising on the spot,
are held in place by hedgerows
winding weeds about their feet.
Trees need their iron echoes
in thoracic x-rayed cages
on the screen of stormy skies,
or their wardrobes for the Spring
will be wasted on the ground
and all their pomp and glory,
saved up for the Summer months,
will pass away uncrowned.

Moment

The silk scarf fell against her face.
She left it there, loving the coolness
and anonymity it gave. It moulded
itself to her, poured all around her,
moving with the sophistry of oil,
sweet-soft as rose petals falling.
Its edges flickered like a flag,
golden yellow, splash of red,
tiny spots of burgundy, of blue.
She stood there in stunned rapture,
as if taken from this earth
in a moment of the greatest joy.

The Sacred Peepal Tree,

ficus religiosa, *in Bihar, India*

The Bodhi tree at Bihar is unwell.
The great Tree of Wisdom,
where Lord Buddha saw the light,
is shedding its springtime leaves
and happiness. Experts will arrive.
Before, it was the mealybug
or carbon soot from candles,
votive tokens by the thousand,
now relegated to a room nearby.
Perhaps the £5 *per* leaf
the monks charge could be the cause
of moral indignation in Gautama.
Or is this a graver warning to the world
from the re-Awakened One?

Peace

I once took time and spent a day
lying on sand just looking up
through tall trees to the canopy.
The sun and sky blinked through,
flickering shafts of clerestorial light.
I stepped out along the sanctuary side.

Sagacities

The navel of the universe,
the pillar of the world,
Buddhist and Hindu,
lie north of Himalayan passes
on the sacred Kailas mountain –
its faces gold, crystal, ruby, blue.
One circuit brings forgiveness
for a lifetime full of sinning.
It is said you may see there
the footprints of the Buddha.

Halfway across the world,
in Southern Africa,
the bearded vulture flies so high
above the Dragon Mountains
it can see into the future.

Night-time

Your night-time breathing stabs so sharply at the air,
a zealot's finger, strident in despair,
expressing what you would not dare reveal
had you remembered someone else was there.
I feel your angry tenseness
as I stare into the darkness.
Fluourescent truths you cannot bear,
burning in that part you will not share.

Peacock at Newnham Courtenay Arboretum, 2 e/

one day with Ted Hughes

A peacock stalked a purple car –
cautious, quizzical, knowing –
quite taken with its own reflection
and the certainty it had a mate.
Throwing up its antique fireguard,
turning to dance on the sandy ground,
it flirted its pram-down feathers
hidden beneath its wedding train.
Now, facing the car, it shimmied
and shook its fan of eyes and dyes.
Suddenly it kissed the car – a thwack –
like a broken belt in a fast machine.
The car screeched in peacockian alarm.

At the Dentist

Buckingham Road, Aylesbury

Being at the dentist is like having a crab
crammed in your face. Stuck like a pike,
choking on a fish too large to swallow –
sheer greed outstripping its desire to live.
The crab's chitinous shell cuts into the corners
of your mouth and its carapace makes you
gag against your palate. The aspirator, meant
to cool the instruments, tries instead to drown
you. The dentist bobs about like a dolphin.
You go home with lips as thick as a whale.

Advert

Very. Sexy. Lady:
the challenge in your look;
the matt-glazed lustre
of your olive eyes;
your languid model-stance;
your self-sufficient air –
all say you've had sex today.
So too your human
half-protective hand
quiescent on your thigh.
Sanctified, you wear white trousers.
Purified, you matched pink pastel
and only ran your fingers
through your hair. Blessed,
you look, quite haughtily, at us,
the less justified, less innocent.

Anasyrma

Look how the moon
lifts her dark skirt
so flagrantly at night
to expose a marble buttock
and bends so boldly
in her own proscenium light.

She is as unconventional
as Venus and Aphrodite
whose acts of revelation
in those antique statutes
the Victorians covered up
like the legs of their pianos.

Or is she more perhaps
like the women in wartime
who raised their skirts
at raw recruits
in the invading army,
to entice and shame them?

What can be her purpose
in mooning the universe
if not to harvest a lover?
Was it the roundness
of her breast or bottom
that made us first idealize?

Perhaps it was the poets
she desired as votaries
to any goddess still
in white, and so preserve
the myth, though man has
breached her thighs.

Here she comes again –
now a net curtain with a wavy bottom,
twitching.

Undressing Fruit

Beneath its pale yellow peel
another skin, a surgery for me –
vellum birch-bark papering the plate.
Blood, dull, magenta glass,
it sprays a musky breath on me –
Mahler's crescendo in his music for dying
which, they say, some people use for love.
It's a performance as tricky
in all its crying, rip and tear
as your poppers, velcro, ties.
For hours I wear that citrus scent
secret on my finger tips,
and, when I come away from you,
relishing the conquest, and the prize.

Getting to know you

I have travelled the long journey of you
from hair tip to toe, I know the route,
have mapped it in my mind, can find
my way again. I have watched the show
on the broad screen of your brow, been led
to the sanctum of your soul. I have seen the vista
from the hill, run the cresta of your hip,
have shared the passage of the nightime ship,
known you open and in secret, the flowers
and the foliage, the rough ground and the smooth,
the laughing places and the shy, your bent toe,
your wrinkled bits. I have watched you sleep
and know the creases where you hide;
held you happy; held you as you cried.

But, though I've travelled and survived,
am I wiser? will I know when I've arrived?

Father

(dates unknown)

I. He left for good when I was 30 months.

I only ever think of him
when other people force me to,
concerned at my indifference.
But he has no shape,
no colour, and no smell,
or anything for me.
He is a void, a concept,
an intellectual thing.
Not a bruise or a smile.
Just an old blue wallet,
two photographs,
and a dozen facts
my mother said were true.
How could he leave two little boys,
one just under five, the other less than three
and never once enquire?
I regret now what he left undone;
hurt, in envy, when I see
a perfect father and a perfect son -
then I cry his love through me.

II. He was born without fingers.

For the stiffness in my hands
          – he had no fingers.
For the way I lean upon my pen
          – he had no fingers.
For the way I tear at broken nails
          – he had no fingers.

For the way I make my half moons beam
        – he had no fingers.
While I can point at all his faults
        – he had no fingers.
I would have proudly held his hand
        –he had no fingers.
He could have clasped me in his arms
        – he had no fingers.

III. Second heart operation.

With the wound he gave his wife
he wounded me not once but twice.
That way he gave the gift of life,
but passed on imperfection too.
Born himself without his fingers
he gave a damaged heart to me
and when he left he broke it too.
I had the damaged heart repaired
in my late twenties, though it stayed
in two. Now at 64, it was becoming one,
but the repair's weakened, come undone.

IV. No father to the boy.

No one to be my hero so I've never worshipped one
No one to set high standards or let me win in games
No one to be my closest friend and urge me on
No one to ruffle up my hair and say 'well done'
No one to forgive mistakes or more grievous wrongs
No one to smile in quiet pride I could easily accept
No one to love and hate intensely in one day
No one to defend me against the world and everyone
No one to slip me extra cash and say 'don't tell Mum'

64

No one to fix my bike or explain how engines worked
No one to discuss ideas and problems, disagree and fight
No one to tell me not to cry, calm down, pull myself together
No one to take that very special care, no rough male kiss at
                                                                night
No father to the boy, so no boy as father to the man.

V. Substitute projection.

I have sought out surrogates all my life, not with intent
but more unconsciously, weighing traits emotionally
in men by instinct with what I did not get at home.
Even those no older than myself have sometimes served me
in this way, bridging gaps, offering a chance, like walking
past a mirror and coming back but finding nothing there
except yourself. Briefly dependent, taken over even,
by a man and friend because he had displayed a hint
of fatherhood, put his hand upon his son in an act of love,
or said perhaps 'I'd never treat a child of mine like that',
when watching something on TV. I find my breath is caught
by such small gestures and remarks, as if a tiny hole is made
into my chest, a single stab thrust very near my heart.
Thus, constantly, my father is a presence in my life. There,
standing over me, me hoping the frown will turn into a smile,
seeking reality in what is just a sad old picture show for me.
Denied, I never called him Father; never called him Dad.

VI. Who was he?

His father hanged himself; he'd mixed two vices:
drink and cards. His mother is a much-creased photograph.
His brother doesn't have a name. Everything I know of him
I have been told, know nothing at first hand. He was a
                                                painter:

murals, pictures, perfume bottles, boxes. He held his brush
between his stubs of fingers, tightly pressed into his palm.
He could not sell his work at home: a silly English prejudice
against the lamed and doubts that he had done it. A linguist,
he lived in France and Italy, forged paintings by the school
at Barbizon. He always drank a lot of Scotch,
crashed cars and drove a wartime ambulance.
He had a tooth moustache; so looked a bit like Hitler.
A snappy dresser judging from the autumn photograph
with his second wife, my mother, promenading loftily
along the esplanade at Hove. Trilby hat; smart overcoat;
gloves to hide his hands. Her, a little plump, hanging on
his arm. Congenial in company, a womaniser, proud,
he had stomach operations; sold his body for research.
I'm told he tried to kill his wife in the Deco entrance hall
at Orpen Road, a rented house they could not justify
or indeed afford. When he left he went abroad;
his lawyer lived in Paris. He sent no love. He sent no money.
He never sent a word. The papers sealing their divorce
came in a plain brown envelope that found its place
behind the dome-topped clock on the mantel near the box
in which my mother kept her silted kidney stone.
That's my father top to toe as far as I can tell or know.

VII. What if he had stayed?

Kafka's father stayed and Kafka hated him:
but that, of course, was Kafka and *his* Dad;
they were about contempt, humiliation, fear.
I forget my father drank a lot, was violent,
self-centred, full of his own ghouls and
senses of unfairness. Would he have been
abusive? It is sad to sense the truth of that.
Pre-teens, I boasted of not needing him
when other children flaunted fathers at me.

Maybe my mother fed the line I was much better
off without him; much better off with her alone.
But because he did not stay, I have no means
of judging just how he might have been.
Absence has forged a brittle archetype of him.

VIII. Old enough to be my father.

One thing my mother told me that I wish I did not know
is that he wanted me to be a girl. She hinted
twice that might have been the reason why he left.
It was, she said, when tall and blonde and beautiful
he could take me out to restaurants and puff with pride
if others said 'It's wrong, he's old enough to be her father'.
That's always seemed pathetic, but in truth it also cut me
to the quick. It put the blame for his rejection not on him,
but me. He has always filled me with a sense of guilt.

IX. He did come back one day (I had forgotten that).

Jacob wrestled with his brother Esau in the womb
to win his birthright. He wrestled with his father
to get his blessing as firstborn. Then he wrestled
with his uncle Laban for his daughters, herds and flocks.
He even wrestled with his God. I wrestled with my father
the one day he came back. I remember I was seven
but my brother, two years older, insists I was eleven.
I have a faded memory of struggling on a single bed.
Was I fighting him as sons fight playfully with their Dads
or was I hoping to prevail and make him stay at home?
I remember too the window, half opaque, partly black.
Jacob wrestled God to solve the problems of his life.
I wrestled with my dark side, and the grey, his deserted wife.
I've not set eyes on him again since he walked out that day.

He only promised me one thing – to take me off to France.
That didn't happen – he failed me as he always had before.
I only ever had in all of mine those three hours of his life.

X. Absence does not make the heart grow fonder.

He did not try; he was not there; he didn't do a thing.
My mother, doing what she did and could, took the brunt
of all my sullen reticence. He was uncaring, feckless, weak.
But absence will not absolve him from his larger share of
                    blame,
though he seems to get off lightly: an echo of an echo in a
                    cave.
He is a void, a concept, an intellectual thing I cannot focus
                    on.
Neither can I find forgetting nor forgiveness in my heart.
The distant longing to be loved he left so undefended
destroyed such virtue; as also any love I ever thought I found.
I shall regret, condemn and punish us while I am still alive,
but, they're nearer to the surface now, not just eating me
                    inside.
Absence has the grimmest face of all the masks of love.

Mother

(1912-1972)

I.

A bit like divorcees with kids
not son and mother, we tolerated
more than loved each other –
You loved you said – too much,
and you exasperated me –
well, that's how it seemed to be.
I was weaned on tins of milk
and left home when I was three,
sent away to stay all week
at the local primary. We were
taught as little adults yet-to-be.
I sat there on my own, self-
absorbed, feeling in the wrong.
Already, I'd run away, aged two,
to the allotment down the road –
Art-Deco Orpen Road in Hove,
where, I'm told, we were fired upon
by a German 'plane that spotted us –
I was in the garden in my pram.
Three years later I packed my bags
but was back again, of course, for tea.
From five I went to boarding school
and for years in summer to a farm –
fed and plucked chickens, drove the cows
(we made them udders-swinging run),
and spied on farmer Ody as he prayed,
peeing against a battered barn.
Once he rodeoed bare-back upon a sow –
I can still see that comic image now.
I ate a whole plate of Mrs Ody's cakes
as a dare, but the 'uncle' took the last

and so I lost the bet. At pre-prep school
another year my birthday cake was given
round – only the crumbs were left for me.
That I so readily recall these things today
shows they are open wounds not fully
healed; soft scabs from early life still there.
Burins bite best on virgin plates, they say.

II.

I got my own back once when cut a piece
of apple pie; I left the slice and took the pie.
I fell for the Odys' lovely niece, Priscilla –
too young and shy, I kept my distance then.
Alone I wandered fields, leaned on gates,
Nature was kind and walked along with me;
she whispered softly in my ear –
I knew Wordsworth before I'd heard
of him, his rhythms and his countryside.
Once we brothers picked the plums
in the orchard of the Angel Inn
at Andover. We made some money,
gorged ourselves relentlessly all day,
crawled back to our halfway-home
and were as sick as dogs all night.
Excess, the burden of our being poor.

III.

One great day when on the farm
you came and took us fishing,
with broomsticks and bent pins,
worms and lengths of string.
We sang so cheerily on the way

70

'Hey ho, hey ho, it's off to work
we go'. We didn't catch a thing.
And were ordered off for fishing
without a licence or permission.
At six I had my first piano lesson.
I can recall the slanting sunlight
that fell across the keys matching
the gold that shone inside of me
thinking you'd found £5 a term
fulfilling my greatest fantasy,
only to learn they'd muddled me
with someone known as Davies III.
I stole a bike and rode the quad
in circles for two hours endlessly,
half in tears and angry with the world.
I recall that blow as if it's only yesterday.
You were a shield to me at the time
of my most serious childhood crime,
taking fountain pens from other boys
who had so much and I did not.
I knew I had done wrong, hid them
in the neighbour's garden; the police
came round. You defended me
from them and back at the school –
I was only ten and didn't have a pen.
I've never found one that works
for me, perfectly: I press too hard.
I wonder what that means? Must we
break things that we've been denied?

IV.

I think you were a bit afraid of me.
I grew up fast with little time
to bridge the gaps my absence

bred, instead they just got wider,
an abyss born of mutual ignorance.
Hugging my hurt I turned into a prig,
a snob, impatient with your wisdom,
which was naive, not culled
like mine from books; learned
for my self-protecting needs.
It didn't help that father left
when I was two; I blamed you
deep inside for driving him away,
a double entered-up rejection
on top of sending me to school
that worked its silent cancer
of deep-dug causes and effects,
building up defences and disdain.
A girlfriend said I had walls of steel
(at least I think that's what she said).
Now, thinking about motherhood,
it's of the role, not you the person –
you're so divorced from what today
is accepted as the norm of 'good'.

V.

Is that too unfair? Perhaps.
But in the broadest terms it's true.
I think you tried to do your best,
did the best that you could do;
taking the 'best' advice you could
(I was assessed by a mason-banker.)
But, it was not 'good enough'
for me, was not what *I* needed.
I was already wounded twice:
my heart imperfect, father gone.
Love was a damaged flower

before it ever bloomed. Love
is best formed in childhood
or it wilts away, forever tainted.
For me it was an instrument
played only by my brain's
left side. It was corrupt
and poisoned me too much,
for far too long. I had no song.
Singing's the voice of love;
I thought in facts not pictures.
My island-ego seemed entire
but my heart became an orphanage.

VI.

You cried when leaving me
at school, each term for years.
I only cried the first time.
My brother 'Tony' misbehaved:
he was too wild for that regime,
and ended exiled to another place.
The strict routine of the school,
now Davids, not Davids II,
suited me. I always read a lot –
I couldn't bear too much reality.
Only later did it dawn on me
there was something selfish
in the way that you behaved.
I thought you had to work;
but you also had to play, and
we were in the way of that. You
had friends, amateur theatricals,
freedom, maybe another man –
there was an 'Uncle Will', in blinds,
who drove a funny three-wheeled van;

we horsed about and nearly tipped it up.
So built up the limbo of our love
that will go on in me forever, fed
by jealousy of rivals for affection.

VII.

But we did explore some closeness
(I do not mean the Oedipal thing:
school was your potent rival there)
until girls and adolescence butted in,
cuddled up in bed to hear the play
on the radio at night each Saturday.
I slept a single pane of glass away
in the 'third room', a glass conservatory,
at the end of the veranda of the flat,
first floor, 179 The Kingsway, Hove,
a building requisitioned by the State
from absent postwar middle classes –
less 'degrading' than the new estates.
My brother slept in a half-curtained
part of the narrow kitchen, opposite
the cooking stove, run on old-style gas.
I felt a bit like a vagrant, tramp –
I hated being a State-supported boy.
You rolled the carpet up to teach
me how to dance (but not too well).
We shared your recitation records
played on a wind-up gramophone
and the doggerel monologues
you gave with such aplomb
to audiences of thousands
mainly at the Dome in Brighton.
The 'Highwayman came riding'
was one of your best turns –

74

I used to test your memory
so you never faltered on the stage.
I giggled in the audience, then left,
in shame, when you were a medium
in your mumbo-jumbo phase.
You ended up a Methodist.
I, unconfirmed, became an atheist:
why should God or the Unconscious
claim or steal my blame or praise?

VIII.

You were running old folks' clubs
in your fancy self-styled hats
made with bases from a Kellogg box
organising others to make the tea,
'mothering' lives that needed you
more than I did by that stage.
You cheered me on if I achieved
though you did not understand:
just what, you asked, is a degree? –
even though you knew I'd spent
three years away at university
it was amazing you didn't know
getting a degree was why I went.
(And you let out my room at home,
the first real space I'd ever had,
one I'd decorated on my own).
Still you had a mother's pride in me
(if you will forgive the pun). It became
a sort of Chinese business wall
between us, annoying me to hell.
Sometimes I couldn't bring myself
to speak to you for hours at a time
if you said something 'out of place'

even when you came to London,
where I lived, on a special visit.
And then your Christian letters
full of emptiness and certainty.
But I cried when you died;
and I cried at the crass cremation
with its melodrama-music,
curtains that drew shuddering;
the rolling platform squeaked
and worked in jerks. There were
two hundred people at the church,
a tribute to you and your life
outside your family. Dr Newman
gave the valediction. I cried
for years at the thought of you,
but now I think it's not for what
we were, but for what we weren't.

IX.

My first birthday came
again for a second time
in nineteen sixty-eight
when I was twenty-six.
I had an operation on
my heart. I was told
I only had four years to live.
I didn't tell you anything.
I couldn't bear or entertain
the thought of your reaction,
your need to claim attention
as you'd waft, gushing,
through the ward. Instead,
I kept quiet, denied a role
to you. I know it hurt and

shocked you, since illness,
yours, like being poor,
was a major binding force
in our family story,
as significant as blood
in others' whom I've known.
Our bond was in adversity.
I denied you in a way
you couldn't comprehend.
But you did not understand
me either: I would have died
of embarrassment and shame.
Now, I must have the op' again,
go back to being one again,
and I am telling everyone.
Peter to Jesus; me to you.

X.

Is this still unfair? It's too easy to forget
the daily duties and concerns, the things
you did and had to undergo for us. Living
on the pittance you received for being ill
when your business fell apart and you
could not run it anymore. I recall that you had
£9 a week for everything. Maybe it was better
I lived away and safe, untroubled, getting on,
courtesy of the Education Act of 1944.
Until I earned my own in holidays, you gave
me spending money, special treats. I loved
to row on the lagoon and go to creaky films
at The Rothbury Cinema in neighbouring Portslade
with threadbare smelly seats; cheap ice-creams;
underage smoke caught in the projector's beam.
Then, there were breaks between the reels

and we raised hell and stamped in unison.
Sometimes I saw the shows through twice
because the second time was free. Or to the roller-
skating rink, whizzing round in hand-held circles,
trying to impress the girls with derring-do.
Or browsing and buying books from the penny box
outside George Hollyman's first shop, him with
his acid-burned bald head, so tall and gruff,
forbidding. But mostly we three walked, learned
to buy the cheapest cuts, found ways of living
on our wits – you could make a meal of anything.
I sold my toys and household bric-à-brac
from boxes on the street, honing salesmen's skills,
went on to sell soap-bars for the blind, earning
twenty-five percent a box, ran a bingo hall,
and ended up a dealer and an auctioneer,
successful in how the world weighs up such things –
tinsel on its crude ill-calibrated scales.

XI

We hid beneath the stairs if the rent man came.
and smoked the ends of other peoples' cigarettes.
No wonder I resented all the tins and tuck
you gave my brother when he joined up
in the merchant navy – you and I had soup
that night and short supplies for weeks.
It symbolised the fate of second sons –
always the hand-me-downs, second-hand.
It didn't do much in terms of feeling special.
I often dressed our docile cat, named Micky,
loved much more than many living things,
trying, maybe, to make another child of him.
In summer it was easier – living on the sea-front
with just a bowling green and then the beach.

I remember all the times I looked out at ships
on the horizon wishing one might bring
my father back, or was it you preventing
him? I didn't know. But swimming, combing
beaches, clambering sea-weed groins was fun,
I was an urchin, running free, half-wind,
almost a creature in Bill Golding's books.
And you were there with food and drinks
and a sort of family life. Then you bought us
bikes and suddenly the countryside was ours -
off we went the three of us, but more and more
I went out on my own, savouring the solitude.
Fractured, family life destroyed its own appeal.

XII.

All this came at a cost to you, you went without
for Anthony and me; we were grateful even then,
knew the family was poor; got used to making do.
But the gap between we two was always there inside.
I lived another life at school. Even young, I knew
I had to manage for myself, be grown up, not rely
on you or anyone. As I got on, gained rank,
achieved at school, the gap became a gulf
for us. I hated visits to the Dachau clothing store
run by the Women's Institute with cast-off clothes
piled high in the local church's hall, the stamps
for points on post-war cards and secret visits
with matron to the linen room where she 'found'
clothes to fit that others would not miss and I
was sworn to silence, made complicit in the 'crime'.
I did become a snob, hated that you came to functions
at the school on a Greenline bus, walked up the drive,
came in homemade clothes that looked homemade
though you'd trained as you proclaimed 'Late West End',

and in the 'fifties got a hundred pounds a gown.
But it was the way you talked so much, 'got on so well'
with other parents, got lifts home, that made me cringe,
made me wish you had not come. For God's sake
you once wrote on a form 'educated in the university
of life!' But, forget all that – for all you did
and all that you denied yourself, I thank you, Mum,
and wish I'd never been deprived of love and had
to think so bad of you in seeking to release myself.
You are a victim of my life, as, in ways, I am of yours.
Our debate will go on while I live. If I can't give you love,
please know I recognise you did do what you did, you tried.
So I guess it is forgive but not forget, I don't hate you
but I can't forget: I live predestined by the ever-real effects
of my first years. They pre-determined almost everything
for me: a driving need for absolute perfection, certainty,
however unachieved; a love of portraits, objects and the dead,
handshaking history, far safer than the chaos that's in lives
and living. But most of all the type of love that I can give
– finite, fragile, furtive, and when rebuffed, withdrawn
without condition. I fight against it, but I can't win through.
You cared: you didn't put me into care, unless we count-in
boarding schools. In your way you were mostly there for me.
I owe you life and the care you gave. I'd hug you if I could.

Note to 'Father' and 'Mother'

These verse sequences or poems virtually wrote themselves almost entirely in September 2006, following the recent discovery that I had to have a second heart operation, a bypass between the ascending and abdominal aorta. In laymen's terms, an aneurism apparently occurred at or soon after the first operation, a coarctation, which had been performed in 1968. Gradually over the years it had silted up and latterly obstructed my aorta, reducing its diameter from 30 to 3 mm. The coarctation itself, found from knotching on my ribcage, had been necessitated by a congenital condition whereby a section of my aorta was entirely shrivelled; that first operation (rather novel at the time) allowed blood to flow through my aorta for the first time in twenty-six years.

The second operation, much more invasive than the first and, I have since been told, one of the largest surgical procedures that can be conceived, was scheduled for 2 November. But after some thirty-eight years of little trouble other than mounting blood pressure from about 2004, I went into hospital as an emergency case on 7 October 2006 and the operation itself was ten days later. My blood pressure reached 260/ 180 [now 140/70] during this period until properly treated with drugs, followed by surgery.

My surgeon, Mr Stephen Westaby, whom I first met on 29 September, had uniquely performed the rare procedure I needed, but only fourteen times. He added though, with the self–assurance appropriate in a surgeon, that he had not lost anyone and implied that he had no intention of losing me. As things turned out, I know that I would have died during October since I was rushed into hospital then, not sometime in the next three or four years of a brain haemorrhage as had been mooted by the physician. Naturally, I handed myself over to the Prof. That I am writing this at all is a testimony to his skill and courage and the support of his impressive surgical team. Incidentally, my heart was 'switched-off' for 37 minutes.

The dedicatees are both Yorkshiremen: Ted Hughes and Stephen Westaby. Ted influenced my inner life more than any other person I have met; the Prof gave me life in which I can try to take forward that influence.

Perhaps I do have two heroes.

Two GPs to whom I am most grateful for their roles in my survival are Doctors Anthony Harnden (for his critical diagnosis and referral; and for his continued care and attention) and Peter Isaac (for his support and timely recommendations) – without them I should not have been in contact with the hospital at all. Dr Jennifer Stein and Dr David Geaney have given me unstinted support, care and understanding, equally important it their way. Dr. Colin Forfar, the consultant cardiologist, had swiftly diagnosed the problem and, though kindly, left me in no doubt of the outcome of inaction – thanks, too, to him.

Whole passages of the poems came straight down my right arm and they were largely complete before the beginning of October. Because of that they have, for me, a certain undeniable integrity; something of what Ted Hughes called 'a language of enactment.' I chose to use details of my life for vitality, rather than metaphor, because I felt the latter might introduce an air of falseness that the subject did not warrant. The works must, of course, be judged on their own merits. They attempt to wrestle with the psychological difficulties of my life, which I knew, in many respects, had acted as hidden motivations for and pre-determinates of my whole existence; they determined that the compromises, restraints and negotiations of marriage were not for me (though I tried it for nine years) and that after 1.4 billion successful years my line has failed to reproduce itself. At one level the poems are about the abusive dimensions of absence. In the face of possible death I felt an over-whelming subliminal need to come to terms with all this and a compulsion to write it down: it was as if my body tacitly informed my mind with an urgency that other circumstances would not have created. I think something similar in him accounts for much of the late flowering of Ted Hughes's genius in his last two years. For me, my confrontations seemed to demand a straight-forward form where energy and honesty informed the narrative. I trust others may find something of value for themselves in what these poems touch on and reveal.

31 January 2007

In Memoriam Bettina Bachmann

We cannot mourn her death.
She lived too well for mourning.

In the logic of the dice
she won against the odds –
bore infirmity, affliction, pain
with resolution and disdain,
earning the awe and honour
of her friends, and of the gods
who sorely sought to test her.
She taught us less is more,
with colours that we saw,
but did not really see. She
had her special style and way,
knew her mind and never feared
to say precisely what she thought
– though deflecting any hurt
with wit and understanding.
In private, quiet, when alone,
in company she shone and
from the disadvantage of her chair
was a magnet everywhere.
Death is not an end for those
we love or much admire.
For they shall be recalled and
quoted, will return in dreams.
With us, they'll always seem alive.
In the democracy of death
she stands out from the crowd.
Let us therefore praise her life.

We cannot mourn her death.
She lived too well for mourning.

RIP R.A.

having met again three months before he was killed.

There we are, the three of us,
standing by chance at a reception;
two in suits, you dressed for Shropshire,
brick trousers, wild hair, no tie.
Fixed under spot lights, glass in hand,
we were a tableau that I photographed
half-consciously. We seemed oddly shy,
embarrassed, almost, to meet again.
Well I was – the one, perhaps like you,
who felt held in least affection, too.
Talking, we pulled in old images,
thoughts, pigeon-holed perceptions,
old prejudgments, challenges of youth,
discords of ancient rivalries.
How much our prime-times flowed,
coming back, refocusing. Slowly,
your bluff good humour spread,
rubbing in its subtle embrocations,
like a full river greeting the sea,
mingling fresh water with saline.
We parted; easier; reassessed –
each allowing the other credit
held in hand before; each claiming
the past with a gentler affection.
Maybe that was your gift,
something I didn't see before.
Now you are no more.
Now, a loss for me.

The Day of Ted's Funeral

North Tawton, Devon

They wrote that the rain drummed down
on the day of your cremation.
That's only partly true. The rain that started
as you were carried from the church
was gentle: soft and silky; smooth
as the finest kaolin slipping through
the fingers of Chinese potters, worried
that fifty years would not be long enough
for their clay to mingle and mature.

It was as if angels were weeping
the first tears of a child,
so fine, so pure, so holy,
they should have been used to baptise
the next baby that was ever born.
All your gentleness in strength,
all your Yorkshire ways, all that
inscape you had found in Nature
were repaid in that evanescent veil.

We stood and watched you driven off.
With our tears, a heavier rain came down.

Doubting Thomases

It was all right for Eliot
in his subvocal sermon
to cast away the human hope
that time might be redeemed –
he'd somewhere else to go.
But we who are remainder
men must claim the present
from the future and the past
and find our fate and fortune
here. Yet, we live too much
defined by what's already gone,
too much the timid creature
in the dark; too governed
by our fear of chance,
and what we've seen of
change, to risk the leap
into a freedom of our own.
It's only on the journey
to the grave that time will
stand aside for us, and the
danger is we leave this life
chained to what we think is safe,
to hopes yet unsecured.
I promise
to go gentle from this world;
at peace with the procession
of all its parts and ages.
Rage is right for burgled youth,
it's not so good for sages.
And death is never more
confused than when we step
ahead and hold the door.
So, may I take my final ride,
when time has died for me,

from a life not mortgaged
to the future and the past.
I want to go through unfenced
open fields with open smiles
from those along the way,
and be so free within myself
to smile at what I had become,
and, at what becomes of me.

Printed by
Short Run Press, Exeter.